Preparative toward a

Natural and Experimental History

by

Francis Bacon

Table of Contents

Description of a Natural and Experimental History Such as May Serve for the Foundation of a True Philosophy

My object in publishing my *Instauration* by parts is that some portion of it may be put out of peril. A similar reason induces me to subjoin here another small portion of the work, and to publish it along with that which has just been set forth. This is the description and delineation of a natural and experimental history, such as may serve to build philosophy upon, and containing material true and copious and aptly digested for the work of the interpreter which follows. The proper place for it would be when I come in due course to the "Preparatives" of Inquiry. I have thought it better, however, to introduce it at once without waiting for that. For a history of this kind, such as I conceive and shall presently describe, is a thing of very great size and cannot be executed without great labor and expense, requiring as it does many people to help, and being (as I have said elsewhere) a kind of royal work. It occurs to me, therefore, that it may not be amiss to try if there be any others who will take these matters in hand, so that while I go on with the completion of my original design, this part which is so manifold and laborious may even during my life (if it so please the Divine Majesty) be prepared and set forth, others applying themselves diligently to it along with me; the rather because my own strength (if I should have no one to help me) is hardly equal to such a province. For as much relates to the work itself of the intellect, I shall perhaps be able to master that by myself; but the materials on which the intellect has to work are so widely spread that one must employ factors and merchants to go everywhere in search of them and bring them in. Besides I hold it to be somewhat beneath the dignity of an undertaking like mine that I should spend my own time in a matter which is open to almost every man's industry. That, however, which is the main part of the matter I will myself now supply, by diligently and exactly setting forth the method and description of a history of this kind, such as shall satisfy my intention; lest men for want of warning set to work the wrong way and guide themselves by the example of the natural histories now in use, and so go far astray from my design. Meanwhile, what I have often said I must here emphatically repeat: that if all the wits of all the ages had met or shall hereafter meet together, if the whole human race had applied or shall hereafter apply themselves to philosophy, and the whole earth had been or shall be nothing but academies and colleges and schools of learned men, still without a natural and experimental history such as I am going to prescribe, no progress worthy of the human race could have been made or can be made in philosophy and the sciences. Whereas, on the other hand, let such a history be once provided and well set forth, and let there be added to it such auxiliary and light-giving experiments as in the very course of interpretation will present themselves or will have to be found out, and the investigation of nature and of all sciences will be the work of a few years. This, therefore, must be done or the business must be given up. For in this way, and in this way only, can the foundations of a true and active philosophy be established; and then will men wake as from deep sleep, and at once perceive what a difference there is between the dogmas and figments of the wit and a true and active philosophy, and what it is in questions of nature to consult nature herself.

First, then, I will give general precepts for the composition of this history; then I will set out the particular figure of it, inserting sometimes as well the purpose to which the inquiry is to be adapted and referred as the particular point to be inquired in order that a good understanding and forecast of the mark aimed at may suggest to men's minds other things also which I may perhaps have overlooked. This history I call "Primary History," or the "Mother History."

Aphorisms on the Composition of the Primary History

I

Nature exists in three states, and is subject, as it were, to three kinds of regimen. Either she is free and develops herself in her own ordinary course, or she is forced out of her proper state by the perverseness and insubordination of matter and the violence of impediments, or she is constrained and molded by art and human ministry. The first state refers to the "species" of things; the second to "monsters"; the third to "things artificial." For in things artificial nature takes orders from man and works under his authority; without man, such things would never have been made. But by the help and ministry of man a new face of bodies, another universe or theater of things, comes into view. Natural history therefore is threefold. It treats of the "liberty" of nature, or the "errors" of nature, or the "bonds" of nature, so that we may fairly distribute it into history of "generations," of "pretergenerations," and of "arts"; which last I also call "mechanical" or "experimental" history. And yet I do not make it a rule that these three should be kept apart and separately treated. For why should not the history of the monsters in the several species be joined with the history of the species themselves? And things artificial again may sometimes be rightly joined with the species, though sometimes they will be better kept separate. It will be best, therefore, to consider these things as the case arises. For too much method produces iterations and prolixity as well as none at all.

II

Natural history, which in its subject (as I said) is threefold, is in its use twofold. For it is used either for the sake of the knowledge of the particular things which it contains or as the primary material of philosophy and the stuff and subject matter of true induction. And it is this latter which is now in hand — now, I say, for the first time; nor has it even been taken in hand till now. For neither Aristotle, nor Theophrastus, nor Dioscorides, nor Gaius Plinius ever set this before them as the end of natural history. And the chief part of the matter rests in this, that they who shall hereafter take it upon them to write natural history should bear this continually in mind — that they ought not to consult the pleasure of the reader, no, nor even that utility which may be derived immediately from their narrations, but to seek out and gather together such store and variety of things as may suffice for the formation of true axioms. Let them but remember this, and they will find out for themselves the method in which the history should be composed. For the end rules the method.

III

But the more difficult and laborious the work is, the more ought it to be discharged of matters superfluous. And therefore there are three things upon which men should be warned to be sparing of their labor, as those which will immensely increase the mass of the work and add little or nothing to its worth.

First then, away with antiquities, and citations or testimonies of authors, and also with disputes and controversies and differing opinions — everything, in short, which is philological. Never cite an author except in a matter of doubtful credit; never introduce a controversy unless in a matter of great moment. And for all that concerns ornaments of speech, similitudes, treasury of eloquence, and such like emptinesses, let it be utterly dismissed. Also let all those things which are admitted be themselves set down briefly and concisely, so that they may be nothing less than words. For no man who is collecting and storing up materials for ship building or the like, thinks of arranging them elegantly, as in a shop, and displaying them so as to please the eye; all his care is that they be sound and good, and that they be so arranged as to take up as little room as possible in the warehouse. And this is exactly what should be done here.

Secondly, that superfluity of natural histories in descriptions and pictures of species, and the curious variety of the same, is not much to the purpose. For small varieties of this kind are only a kind of sports and wanton freaks of nature and come near to the nature of individuals. They afford a pleasant recreation in wandering among them and looking at them as objects in themselves, but the information they yield to the sciences is slight and almost superfluous.

Thirdly, all superstitious stories (I do not say stories of prodigies, when the report appears to be faithful and probable, but superstitious stories) and experiments of ceremonial magic should

9

be altogether rejected. For I would not have the infancy of philosophy, to which natural history is as a nursing mother, accustomed to old wives' fables. The time will perhaps come (after we have gone somewhat deeper into the investigation of nature) for a light review of things of this kind, that if there remain any grains of natural virtue in these dregs, they may be extracted and laid up for use. In the meantime they should be set aside. Even the experiments of natural magic should be sifted diligently and severely before they are received, especially those which are commonly derived from vulgar sympathies and antipathies, with great sloth and facility both of believing and inventing.

And it is no small thing to relieve natural history from the three superfluities above mentioned, which would otherwise fill volumes. Nor is this all. For in a great work it is no less necessary that what is admitted should be written succinctly than that what is superfluous should be rejected, though no doubt this kind of chastity and brevity will give less pleasure both to the reader and the writer. But it is always to be remembered that this which we are now about is only a granary and storehouse of matters, not meant to be pleasant to stay or live in, but only to be entered as occasion requires, when anything is wanted for the work of the interpreter which follows.

IV

In the history which I require and design, special care is to be taken that it be of wide range and made to the measure of the universe. For the world is not to be narrowed till it will go into the understanding (which has been done hitherto), but the understanding to be expanded and opened till it can take in the image of the world as it is in fact. For that fashion of taking few things into account, and pronouncing with reference to a few things, has been the ruin of everything. To resume then the divisions of natural history which I made just now — viz., that it is a history of generations, Pretergenerations, and arts — I divide the history of generations into five parts. The first, of ether and things celestial. The second, of meteors and the regions (as they call them) of air, viz., of the tracts which lie between the moon and the surface of the earth; to which part also (for order's sake, however the truth of the thing may be) I assign comets of whatever kind, both higher and lower. The third, of earth and sea. The fourth, of the elements (as they call them), flame or fire, air, water, earth, understanding, however, by elements, not the first principles of things, but the greater masses of natural bodies. For the nature of things is so distributed that the quantity or mass of some bodies in the universe is very great, because their configurations require a texture of matter easy and obvious, such as are those four bodies which I have mentioned; while of certain other bodies the quantity is small and weakly supplied, because the texture of matter which they require is very complex and subtle, and for the most part determinate and organic, such as are the species of natural things — metals, plants, animals. Hence I call the former kind of bodies the "greater colleges," the latter the "lesser colleges." Now the fourth part of the history is of those greater colleges — under the name of elements, as I said. And let it not be thought that I confound this fourth part with the second and third, because in each of them I have mentioned air, water, and earth. For the history of these enters into the second and third, as they are integral parts of the world, and as they relate to the fabric and configuration of the universe. But in the fourth is contained the history of their own substance and nature, as it exists in their several parts of uniform structure, and without reference to the whole. Lastly, the fifth part of the history contains the lesser colleges, or species, upon which natural history has hitherto been principally employed.

As for the history of pretergenerations, I have already said that it may be most conveniently joined with the history of generations — I mean the history of prodigies which are natural. For the superstitious history of marvels (of whatever kind) I remit to a quite separate treatise of its own; which treatise I do not wish to be undertaken now at first, but a little after, when the investigation of nature has been carried deeper.

History of arts, and of nature as changed and altered by man, or experimental history, I divide into three. For it is drawn either from mechanical arts, or from the operative part of the liberal arts, or from a number of crafts and experiments which have not yet grown into an art properly so called, and which sometimes indeed turn up in the course of most ordinary experience and do not stand at all in need of art.

As soon, therefore, as a history has been completed of all these things which I have mentioned — namely, generations, pretergenerations, arts, and experiments, it seems that nothing will remain unprovided whereby the sense can be equipped for information of the understanding. And then shall we be no longer kept dancing within little rings, like persons bewitched, but our range and circuit will be as wide as the compass of the world.

V

Among the parts of history which I have mentioned, the history of arts is of most use because it exhibits things in motion and leads more directly to practice. Moreover, it takes off the mask and veil from natural objects, which are commonly concealed and obscured under the variety of shapes and external appearance. Finally, the vexations of art are certainly as the bonds and handcuffs of Proteus, which betray the ultimate struggles and efforts of matter. For bodies will not be destroyed or annihilated, rather than that they will turn themselves into various forms. Upon this history, therefore, mechanical and illiberal as it may seem (all fineness and daintiness set aside), the greatest diligence must be bestowed.

Again, among the particular arts those are to be preferred which exhibit, alter, and prepare natural bodies and materials of things, such as agriculture, cookery, chemistry, dyeing, the manufacture of glass, enamel, sugar, gunpowder, artificial fires, paper, and the like. Those which consist principally in the subtle motion of the hands or instruments are of less use, such as weaving, carpentry, architecture, manufacture of mills, clocks, and the like, although these too are by no means to be neglected, both because many things occur in them which relate to the alterations of natural bodies, and because they give accurate information concerning local motion, which is a thing of great importance in very many respects.

But in the whole collection of this history of arts it is especially to be observed and constantly borne in mind that not only those experiments in each art which serve the purpose of the art itself are to be received, but likewise those which turn up anyhow by the way. For example, that locusts or crabs, which were before of the color of mud, turn red when baked is nothing to the table; but this very instance is not a bad one for investigating the nature of redness, seeing that the same thing happens in baked bricks. In like manner the fact that meat is sooner salted in winter than in summer is not only important for the cook that he may know how to regulate the pickling, but is likewise a good instance for showing the nature and impression of cold. Therefore, it would be an utter mistake to suppose that my intention would be satisfied by a collection of experiments of arts made only with the view of thereby bringing the several arts to greater perfection. For though this be an object which in many cases I do not despise, yet my meaning plainly is that all mechanical experiments should be as streams flowing from all sides into the sea of philosophy. But how to select the more important instances in every kind (which are principally and with the greatest diligence to be sought and as it were hunted out) is a point to be learned from the prerogatives of instances.

VI

In this place also is to be resumed that which in the 99th, 119th, and 120th aphorisms of the first book I treated more at large, but which it may be enough here to enjoin shortly by way of precept — namely, that there are to be received into this history, first, things the most ordinary, such as it might be thought superfluous to record in writing because they are so familiarly known; secondly, things mean, illiberal, filthy (for "to the pure all things are pure," and if money obtained from Vespasian's tax smelt well, much more does light and information from whatever source derived); thirdly, things trifling and childish (and no wonder, for we are to become again as little children); and lastly, things which seem over subtle, because they are in themselves of no use. For the things which will be set forth in this history are not collected (as I have already said) on their own account; and therefore neither is their importance to be measured by what they are worth in themselves, but according to their indirect bearing upon other things and the influence they may have upon philosophy.

VII

Another precept is that everything relating both to bodies and virtues in nature be set forth (as far as may be) numbered, weighed, measured, defined. For it is works we are in pursuit of, not speculations; and practical working comes of the due combination of physics and mathematics. And therefore the exact revolutions and distances of the planets — in the history of the heavenly bodies; the compass of the land and the superficial space it occupies in comparison of the waters — in the history of earth and sea; how much compression air will bear without strong resistance — in the history of air; how much one metal outweighs another — in the history of metals; and numberless other particulars of that kind are to be ascertained and set down. And when exact proportions cannot be obtained, then we must have recourse to indefinite estimates and comparatives. As for instance (if we happen to distrust the calculations of astronomers as to the distances of the planets), that the moon is within the shadow of the earth, that Mercury is beyond the moon, and the like. Also when mean proportions cannot be had, let extremes be proposed, as that a weak magnet will raise so many times its own weight of iron, while the most powerful will raise sixty times its own weight (as I have myself seen in the case of a very small armed magnet). I know well enough that these definite instances do not occur readily or often, but that they must be sought for as auxiliaries in the course of interpretation itself when they are most wanted. But nevertheless if they present themselves accidentally, provided they do not too much interrupt the progress of the natural history, they should also be entered therein.

VIII

With regard to the credit of the things which are to be admitted into the history, they must needs be either certainly true, doubtful whether true or not, or certainly not true. Things of the first kind should be set down simply; things of the second kind with a qualifying note, such as "it is reported," "they relate," "I have heard from a person of credit," and the like. For to add the arguments on either side would be too laborious and would certainly interrupt the writer too much. Nor is it of much consequence to the business in hand because (as I have said in the 118th aphorism of the first book) mistakes in experimenting, unless they abound everywhere, will be presently detected and corrected by the truth of axioms. And yet if the instance be of importance, either from its own use or because many other things may depend upon it, then certainly the name of the author should be given, and not the name merely, but it should be mentioned withal whether he took it from report, oral or written (as most of Pliny's statements are), or rather affirmed it of his own knowledge; also whether it was a thing which happened in his own time or earlier; and again, whether it was a thing of which, if it really happened, there must needs have been many witnesses; and finally, whether the author was a vain-speaking and light person or sober and severe; and the like points, which bear upon the weight of the evidence. Lastly, things which though certainly not true are yet current and much in men's mouths, having either through neglect or from the use of them in similitudes prevailed now for many ages (as that the diamond binds the magnet, garlic weakens it, that amber attracts everything except basil, and other things of that kind), these it will not be enough to reject silently; they must be in express words proscribed, that the sciences may be no more troubled with them.

Besides, it will not be amiss, when the source of any vanity or credulity happens to present itself, to make a note of it, as, for example, that the power of exciting Venus is ascribed to the herb

Satyrion because its root takes the shape of testicles — when the real cause of this is that a fresh bulbous root grows upon it every year, last year's root still remaining; whence those twin bulbs. And it is manifest that this is so, because the new root is always found to be solid and succulent, the old withered and spongy. And therefore it is no marvel if one sinks in water and the other swims — which nevertheless goes for a wonder and has added credit to the other virtues ascribed to this herb.

IX

There are also some things which may be usefully added to the natural history, and which will make it fitter and more convenient for the work of the interpreter, which follows. They are five.

First, questions (I do not mean as to causes but as to the fact) should be added in order to provoke and stimulate further inquiry, as in the history of earth and sea, whether the Caspian ebbs and flows, and at how many hours' interval; whether there is any southern continent or only islands, and the like.

Secondly, in any new and more subtle experiment the manner in which the experiment was conducted should be added, that men may be free to judge for themselves whether the information obtained from that experiment be trustworthy or fallacious, and also that men's industry may be roused to discover, if possible, methods more exact.

Thirdly, if in any statement there be anything doubtful or questionable, I would by no means have it suppressed or passed in silence, but plainly and perspicuously set down by way of note or admonition. For I want this primary history to be compiled with a most religious care, as if every particular were stated upon oath, seeing that it is the book of God's works and (so far as the majesty of heavenly may be compared with the humbleness of earthly things) a kind of second Scripture.

Fourthly, it would not be amiss to intersperse observations occasionally, as Pliny has done; as in the history of earth and sea, that the figure of the earth (as far as it is yet known) compared with the seas is narrow and pointed toward the south, wide and broad toward the north, the figure of the sea contrary; that the great oceans intersect the earth in channels running north and south, not east and west, except perhaps in the extreme polar regions. It is also very good to add canons (which are nothing more than certain general and catholic observations), as in the history of the heavenly bodies, that Venus is never distant more than 46 parts from the sun, Mercury never more than 23, and that the planets which are placed above the sun move slowest when they are furthest from the earth, those under the sun fastest. Moreover, there is another kind of observation to be employed, which has not yet come into use, though it be of no small importance. This is, that to the enumeration of things which are should be subjoined an enumeration of things which are not. As in the history of the heavenly bodies, that there is not found any star oblong or triangular, but that every star is globular — either globular simply, as the moon, or apparently angular, but globular in the middle, as the other stars, or apparently radiant but globular in the middle, as the sun — or that the stars are scattered about the sky in no order at all, so that there is not found among them either quincunx or square, or any other regular figure (howsoever the names be given of Delta, Crown, Cross, Chariot, etc.) scarcely so much as a straight line, except perhaps in the belt and dagger of Orion.

Fifthly, that may perhaps be of some assistance to an inquirer which is the ruin and destruction of a believer; viz., a brief review, as in passage, of the opinions now received, with their varieties and sects, that they may touch and rouse the intellect and no more.

X

And this will be enough in the way of general precepts which, if they be diligently observed, the work of the history will at once go straight toward its object and be prevented from increasing beyond bounds. But if even as here circumscribed and limited it should appear to some poor-spirited person a vast work — let him turn to the libraries; and there among other things let him look at the bodies of civil and canonical law on one side, and at the commentaries of doctors and lawyers on the other, and see what a difference there is between the two in point of mass and volume. For we (who as faithful secretaries do but enter and set down the laws themselves of nature and nothing else) are content with brevity, and almost compelled to it by the condition of things; whereas opinions, doctrines, and speculations are without number and without end.

And whereas in the Plan of the Work I have spoken of the *cardinal virtues* in nature, and said that a history of these must also be collected and written before we come to the work of Interpretation, I have not forgotten this, but I reserve this part for myself since until men have begun to be somewhat more closely intimate with nature, I cannot venture to rely very much on other people's industry in that matter.

And now should come the delineation of the particular histories. But I have at present so many other things to do that I can only find time to subjoin a Catalogue of their titles. As soon, however, as I have leisure for it, I mean to draw up a set of questions on the several subjects, and to explain what points with regard to each of the histories are especially to be inquired and collected, as conducing to the end I have in view — like a kind of particular topics. In other words, I mean (according to the practice in civil causes) in this great plea or suit granted by the divine favor and providence (whereby the human race seeks to recover its right over nature), to examine nature herself and the arts upon interrogatories.

CATALOGUE OF PARTICULAR HISTORIES BY TITLES

1. History of the Heavenly Bodies; or Astronomical History.

2. History of the Configuration of the Heaven and the parts thereof toward the Earth and the parts thereof; or Cosmographical History.

3. History of Comets.

4. History of Fiery Meteors.

5. History of Lightnings, Thunderbolts, Thunders, and Coruscations.

6. History of Winds and Sudden Blasts and Undulations of the Air.

7. History of Rainbows.

8. History of Clouds, as they are seen above.

9. History of the Blue Expanse, of Twilight, of Mock-Suns, Mock-Moons, Haloes, various colors of the Sun; and of every variety in the aspect of the heavens caused by the medium.

10. History of Showers, Ordinary, Stormy, and Prodigious; also of Waterspouts (as they are called); and the like.

11. History of Hail, Snow, Frost, Hoar-frost, Fog, Dew, and the like.

12. History of all other things that fall or descend from above, and that are generated in the upper region.

13. History of Sounds in the upper region (if there be any), besides Thunder.

14. History of Air as a whole, or in the Configuration of the World.

15. History of the Seasons or Temperatures of the Year, as well according to the variations of Regions as according to accidents of Times and periods of Years; of Floods, Heats, Droughts, and the like.

16. History of Earth and Sea; of the Shape and Compass of them, and their Configurations compared with each other; and of their broadening or narrowing; of Islands in the Sea; of Gulfs of the Sea, and Salt Lakes within the Land; Isthmuses and Promontories.

17. History of the Motions (if any be) of the Globe of Earth and Sea; and of the Experiments from which such motions may be collected.

18. History of the greater Motions and Perturbations in Earth and Sea; Earthquakes, Tremblings and Yawnings of the Earth, Islands newly appearing; Floating Islands; Breakings off of Land by entrance of the Sea, Encroachments and Inundations and contrariwise Recessions of the Sea; Eruptions of Fire from the Earth; Sudden Eruptions of Waters from the Earth; and the like.

19. Natural History of Geography; of Mountains, Valleys, Woods, Plains, Sands, Marshes, Lakes, Rivers, Torrents, Springs, and every variety of their course, and the like; leaving apart Nations, Provinces, Cities, and such like matters pertaining to Civil life.

20. History of Ebbs and Flows of the Sea; Currents, Undulations, and other Motions of the Sea.

21. History of the other Accidents of the Sea; its Saltness, its various Colors, its Depth; also of Rocks, Mountains and Valleys under the Sea, and the like.

Next come Histories of the Greater Masses.

22. History of Flame and of things Ignited.

23. History of Air, in Substance, not in the Configuration of the World.

24. History of Water, in Substance, not in the Configuration of the World.

25. History of Earth and the diversity thereof, in Substance, not in the Configuration of the World.

Next come Histories of Species.

26. History of perfect Metals, Gold, Silver; and of the Mines, Veins, Marcasites of the same; also of the Working in the Mines.

27. History of Quicksilver.

28. History of Fossils; as Vitriol, Sulphur, etc.

29. History of Gems; as the Diamond, the Ruby, etc.

30. History of Stones; as Marble, Touchstone, Flint, etc.

31. History of the Magnet.

32. History of Miscellaneous Bodies, which are neither entirely Fossil nor Vegetable; as Salts, Amber, Ambergris, etc.

33. Chemical History of Metals and Minerals.

34. History of Plants, Trees, Shrubs, Herbs; and of their parts, Roots, Stalks, Wood, Leaves, Flowers, Fruits, Seeds, Gums, etc.

35. Chemical History of Vegetables.

36. History of Fishes, and the Parts and Generation of them.

37. History of Birds, and the Parts and Generation of them.

38. History of Quadrupeds, and the Parts and Generation of them.

39. History of Serpents, Worms, Flies, and other insects; and of the Parts and Generation of them.

40. Chemical History of the things which are taken by Animals.

Next come Histories of Man.

41. History of the Figure and External Limbs of Man, his Stature, Frame, Countenance and Features; and of the variety of the same according to Races and Climates, or other smaller differences.

42. Physiognomical History of the same.

43. Anatomical History, or of the Internal Members of Man; and of the variety of them, as it is found in the Natural Frame and Structure, and not merely as regards Diseases and Accidents out of the course of Nature.

44. History of the parts of Uniform Structure in Man; as Flesh, Bones, Membranes, etc.

45. History of Humors in Man; Blood, Bile, Seed, etc.

46. History of Excrements; Spittle, Urine, Sweats, Stools, Hair of the Head, Hairs of the Body, Whitlows, Nails, and the like.

47. History of Faculties; Attraction, Digestion, Retention, Expulsion, Sanguification, Assimilation of Aliment into the members, conversion of Blood and Flower of Blood into Spirit, etc.

48. History of Natural and Involuntary Motions; as Motion of the Heart, the Pulses, Sneezing, Lungs, Erection, etc.

49. History of Motions partly Natural and partly Violent; as of Respiration, Cough, Urine, Stool, etc.

50. History of Voluntary Motions; as of the Instruments of Articulation of Words; Motions of the Eyes, Tongue, Jaws, Hands, Fingers; of Swallowing, etc.

51. History of Sleep and Dreams.

52. History of different habits of Body — Fat, Lean; of the Complexions (as they call them), etc.

53. History of the Generation of Man.

54. History of Conception, Vivification, Gestation in the Womb, Birth, etc.

55. History of the Food of Man; and of all things Eatable and Drinkable; and of all Diet; and of the variety of the same according to nations and smaller differences.

56. History of the Growth and Increase of the Body, in the whole and in its parts.

57. History of the Course of Age; Infancy, Boyhood, Youth, Old Age; of Length and Shortness of Life, and the like, according to nations and lesser differences.

58. History of Life and Death.

59. History Medicinal of Diseases, and the Symptoms and Signs of them.

60. History Medicinal of the Treatment and Remedies and Cures of Diseases.

61. History Medicinal of those things which preserve the Body and the Health.

62. History Medicinal of those things which relate to the Form and Comeliness of the Body.

63. History Medicinal of those things which alter the Body, and pertain to Alternative Regimen.

64. History of Drugs.

65. History of Surgery.

66. Chemical History of Medicines.

67. History of Vision, and of things Visible.

68. History of Painting, Sculpture, Modelling, etc.

69. History of Hearing and Sound.

70. History of Music.

71. History of Smell and Smells.

72. History of Taste and Tastes.

73. History of Touch, and the objects of Touch.

74. History of Venus, as a species of Touch.

75. History of Bodily Pains, as species of Touch.

76. History of Pleasure and Pain in general.

77. History of the Affections; as Anger, Love, Shame, etc.

78. History of the Intellectual Faculties; Reflection, Imagination, Discourse, Memory, etc.

79. History of Natural Divinations.

80. History of Diagnostics, or Secret Natural Judgments.

81. History of Cookery, and the arts thereto belonging, as of the Butcher, Poulterer, etc.

82. History of Baking, and the Making of Bread, and the arts thereto belonging, as of the Miller, etc.

83. History of Wine.

84. History of the Cellar and of different kinds of Drink.

85. History of Sweetmeats and Confections.

86. History of Honey.

87. History of Sugar.

88. History of the Dairy.

89. History of Baths and Ointments.

90. Miscellaneous History concerning the care of the body — as of Barbers, Perfumers, etc.

91. History of the working of Gold, and the arts thereto belonging.

92. History of the manufactures of Wool, and the arts thereto belonging.

93. History of the manufactures of Silk, and the arts thereto belonging.

94. History of manufactures of Flax, Hemp, Cotton, Hair, and other kinds of Thread, and the arts thereto belonging.

95. History of manufactures of Feathers.

96. History of Weaving, and the arts thereto belonging.

97. History of Dyeing.

98. History of Leather-making, Tanning, and the arts thereto belonging.

99. History of Ticking and Feathers.

100. History of working in Iron.

101. History of Stone-cutting.

102. History of the making of Bricks and Tiles.

103. History of Pottery.

104. History of Cements, etc.

105. History of working in Wood.

106. History of working in Lead.

107. History of Glass and all vitreous substances, and of Glass-making.

108. History of Architecture generally.

109. History of Wagons, Chariots, Litters, etc.

110. History of Printing, of Books, of Writing, of Sealing; of Ink, Pen, Paper, Parchment, etc.

111. History of Wax.

112. History of Basket-making.

113. History of Mat-making, and of manufactures of Straw, Rushes, and the like.

114. History of Washing, Scouring, etc.

115. History of Agriculture, Pasturage, Culture of Woods, etc.

116. History of Gardening.

117. History of Fishing.

118. History of Hunting and Fowling.

119. History of the Art of War, and of the arts thereto belonging, as Armory, Bow-making, Arrow-making, Musketry, Ordnance, Cross-bows, Machines, etc.

120. History of the Art of Navigation, and of the crafts and arts thereto belonging.

121. History of Athletics and Human Exercises of all kinds.

122. History of Horsemanship.

123. History of Games of all kinds.

124. History of Jugglers and Mountebanks.

125. Miscellaneous History of various Artificial Materials, — as Enamel, Porcelain, various Cements, etc.

126. History of Salts.

127. Miscellaneous History of various Machines and Motions.

128. Miscellaneous History of Common Experiments which have not grown into an Art.

Histories must also be written of Pure Mathematics; though they are rather observations than experiments.

129. History of the Natures and Powers of Numbers.

130. History of the Natures and Powers of Figures.

It may not be amiss to observe that, whereas many of the experiments must come under more titles than one (as the history of plants and the history of the art of gardening have many things in common), it will be more convenient to investigate them with reference to arts, and to arrange them with reference to bodies. For I care little about the mechanical arts themselves: only about those things which they contribute to the equipment of philosophy. But these things will be better regulated as the case arises.